YOUR KNOWLEDGE HAS VALUE

- We will publish your bachelor's and master's thesis, essays and papers

- Your own eBook and book - sold worldwide in all relevant shops

- Earn money with each sale

Upload your text at www.GRIN.com and publish for free

Bibliographic information published by the German National Library:

The German National Library lists this publication in the National Bibliography; detailed bibliographic data are available on the Internet at http://dnb.dnb.de .

This book is copyright material and must not be copied, reproduced, transferred, distributed, leased, licensed or publicly performed or used in any way except as specifically permitted in writing by the publishers, as allowed under the terms and conditions under which it was purchased or as strictly permitted by applicable copyright law. Any unauthorized distribution or use of this text may be a direct infringement of the author s and publisher s rights and those responsible may be liable in law accordingly.

Imprint:

Copyright © 2018 GRIN Verlag
Print and binding: Books on Demand GmbH, Norderstedt Germany
ISBN: 9783668688810

This book at GRIN:

https://www.grin.com/document/421540

Victor Rodney

Decline of African Americans in Baseball

GRIN Verlag

GRIN - Your knowledge has value

Since its foundation in 1998, GRIN has specialized in publishing academic texts by students, college teachers and other academics as e-book and printed book. The website www.grin.com is an ideal platform for presenting term papers, final papers, scientific essays, dissertations and specialist books.

Visit us on the internet:

http://www.grin.com/

http://www.facebook.com/grincom

http://www.twitter.com/grin_com

Contents

Introduction/Background 1

Wealth and population size 2

Community and family support 3

Racism 4

Solution to the remedy 6

Conclusion 7

Decline of African Americans in Baseball

Introduction/Background

In American sports, Baseball seems to be affected by the decrease in the number of African-American players. The baseball is a game that has been appreciated by many across America and beyond. Having the Africans out of the game is worrying issues since this might be taken as racial discrimination. This decline was started being a notice in the 70s through 80s and the issue seems to worsen in the nineties. In the past years, the number of African Americans was always highest. The number of African American players records a decline of eighteen percent an issue some researchers are working hard to hide and give a false number of 26 percentages.

The decline happened after the celebration of Jackie Robinson win, which was celebrated by many. By this time, Latinos were not too much involved in sports. As the time went by, the Latinos started increasing and showing they are interested in sports while the number of African Americans declined (Klein, p. 190). Up to now, there is no research that is able to explain clearly the reason for the decline. In this paper, I will argue the possible ways that led to the decline of African American and how it can be revived.

1

Wealth and population size

I believe the population is the major root cause of the decline of African American in Baseball. Of late Latino players have recorded a massive increase in Baseball than African Americans players. This is one of the factors that have contributed to the decline. However, the fact remains the Latinos are almost equal to African Americans in terms of population. Initially, the Latinos were not as many compared to African American players in baseball and in the country. The Latino population compared to African America does not have much difference as the one in the figure playing baseball (Baseball Demographics, p. 2000). This makes us shift our mind from population issue to wealth that is dependent on what each one earns. In terms of making a good amount of money, the whites are known to have good earnings compared to blacks. Baseball is an involving and demanding sport, which requires a lot of investments. Compared to the whites, blacks do not earn good amount of money and therefore they opt to shift to other sports that are not demanding (Oliver, Melvin, and Thomas, p. 1).

When joining colleges, the students are required to contribute a certain amount of money as registration fees and in between, there are other amounts of money needed to run the sport. This becomes a burden to Africans who cannot afford to raise such amount of money required in baseball and they end up on other sports. This becomes a discouraging factor has led to the decline of African American baseball players.

Whites are favored in jobs more than the Africans America and therefore raising money is not a big issue to them than it is with the blacks. To African Americans, money hinders them from having an equal competition with the whites. To form a game, baseball requires a large group of participants and therefore there is a need for baseball fields, league and other facilities that are not locally available.

Therefore, it becomes easier to register Latin American than African America talents and gloom them at several academies major leagues. This resulted in the increase of Latin American and a decrease of African American in Baseball.

Community and family support

Baseball, unlike other sports, required regular tournaments. This is the only ways baseball players showcase their talents. Baseball requires great community and family involvement unlike other sports (Hodge, p. 930). This is another arguable fact why African American baseball declined. College and community are an area that has a high chance of influencing players. Baseball, unlike other sports, is not easy to organize a league or a tournament and therefore funds are needed. If the families of the team players are not concerned or are not financially stable to support the sport, it, therefore, means that the player will be left with no other option other than leaving for another sport if s\he lack financial support. The weekly sports organized by the school serves as a significant social gathering and plays a major part in popularizing the sport.

If the school lacks funds to organize for the weekly tournament, the popularity of the sport will go down by far (Open-organizations, p. 1). The same case applies to the community. If they lack resources to fund the youth tournaments as well as the travel leagues for exceptional adolescents, then the baseball players will not have the opportunity to play baseball. This is clearly, what happened to African American baseball player. They lacked the community support to fund them for leagues and there were no opportunities to play, unlike the whites where the community supported them well. Moreover, due to lack of exposure, the African American lacked interest in Baseball and that is where they are recording a decline in baseball sports.

Family support very important in baseball sport. Family participation in baseball sport may be highly required due to financial support in a Baseball organization. The cost demanded is for baseball is high compared to other sports and therefore the unity and support is highly required. If a rift happens to occurs that may hinder the family support, the player may be left with no other option other than to drop out of the sport. This generally happens to African American. The rate by which black families in America divorces are high and this affects black players.

Racism

Researchers argue that the decline is not highly affected by racial basis but it is evident that White players are prioritized in baseball sports. The baseball requires a big but not bigger number of participants and therefore it may not have a chance for everyone to participate in the league on a particular day. Participants are chosen among a large number of players and this is where racism occurs. The couch managing the sport give high chances to white players than Africans and this makes the African Americans lose interest in the sport.

After the celebration of Jackie Robinson, the white started creating rifts with blacks and they did not want to hear any black player on the team (Lanctot, p. 1). They claimed that there are not there to be drafted. This led to the decline in African American baseball players.

School initiative

In most of the middle and higher schools, baseball is supported which makes difference in youth sports opportunities that are not offered outside. Football and basketballs are the most played and appreciated in most high schools and colleges (Pedroni, p.1). To become unique in sports, some schools adopted baseball as a unique sport that will unite and give opportunities to the youth having talents in baseball and athletics. There is collaboration with high school coaches and college coaches in encouraging which school to attend. The recruiter may offer a favor to coaches, which might not be offed by MLB scouts.

Schools recruit's referral students into baseball organizations with the school leaving the large and willing number out. Therefore, when the African American finishes the school, they are in a hurry to join employment leaving the whites in baseball sports. After being employed, the blacks' abandons athletics since it is of no use to them.

I also wondered why most the African Americans get interested in football sports more than they are in other sports. It is factual that football sports, unlike baseball, they appreciate every team player despite the race, ethnic or even class. Most of the schools offer sport as a major sport since it will have more participants than other sports and the more the participant, the more the sweeter the sport becomes (Open-organizations, p.1). In football, a student starts getting paid as early as they start participating in tournaments, unlike baseball where you can stay for years without starting earning some money.

Solution to the remedy

To regain the spirit of African American baseball player, equity among whites and blacks must be observed keenly. African Americans feel down looked by the whites who are given more priority than black. This really discourages them to participate in any baseball game thus resulting them to quit to other activities where they will be appreciated. When the African Americans win against whites, this becomes a problem when enmity starts growing since whites want to remain superior in everything forgetting that others are talents and can perform even better if they are given chances.

It is true if the coaches cease to be tribal and racial, the African America baseball team can come back strong than ever. Baseball is a talent, not a forced activity that can be done by everyone. Therefore, an equal opportunity should be given to Africans American as it is with the whites.

Communities should support the youth leagues despite the color to regain the beauty of baseball sport. Community in America supported their own whites more than they did to Africans leading to the isolation of talented Africans Americans. For fair competition in sports, all participant should be viewed as a player and not based on their skin color.

American have noticed the decrease and initiated two programs, which are believed it will have an impact in the effort of restoring back African American baseball players as they were earlier. The two major programs are RBI (Reviving baseball in inner cities) and the Urban Youth Academy (Lanctot, p. 1). RBI has spread to 200 cities worldwide with a range of more than 250,000 participants. The Urban Youth Academy was founded in 2006 with an aim of offering equal opportunities to the youth of all races to play baseball.

Conclusion

The major decline of African American baseball player is of more concern than a catastrophe. The leading baseball organization all over is trying all they can to restore back the African America into sports. In addition, they have set organizations to cater for this problem, which we hope it will succeed in reviving back African American into baseball sports. There should be a concrete guarantee that African Americans will be served equally to whites in baseball sports as well as other sports.

Work cited

Hodge, Samuel R., et al. "Brown in Black and White—Then and now: A question of educating or sporting African American males in America." *American Behavioral Scientist* 51.7 (2008): 928-952.

Klein, A. "Transnationalism, Labour Migration and Latin American Baseball'." *The global sports arena: Athletic talent migration in an interdependent world* (2013): 183-205.

Lanctot, Neil. *Negro league baseball: The rise and ruin of a Black institution.* University of Pennsylvania Press, 2011.

Pedroni, Thomas C. *Market movements: African American involvement in school voucher reform.* Routledge, 2013.

Oliver, Melvin, and Thomas Shapiro. *Black wealth/white wealth: A new perspective on racial inequality.* Routledge, 2013.

"Baseball Demographics, 1947-2016." *Baseball Demographics, 1947-2016 | Society for American Baseball Research*, sabr.org/bioproj/topic/baseball-demographics-1947-2012.

Open-organizations http://www.open-organizations.org/decline-of-african-americans-in-baseball-an-essay-sample/ (accessed Apr 16, 2018).

YOUR KNOWLEDGE HAS VALUE

- We will publish your bachelor's and
  master's thesis, essays and papers

- Your own eBook and book -
  sold worldwide in all relevant shops

- Earn money with each sale

Upload your text at www.GRIN.com
and publish for free